The Healed Heart of Christmas

Esther C. Baird

The Healed Heart of Christmas
© Esther C. Baird
2023
www.estherbaird.com
All rights reserved.

Unless otherwise indicated, all Scripture quotations are taken from the *Holy Bible*, New Living Translation, copyright © 1996, 2004, 2015 by Tyndale House Foundation. Used by permission of Tyndale House Publishers, Inc., Carol Stream, Illinois 60188. All rights reserved.

ISBN: 9798862036954

Cover Design: Andrew Runion

CONTENTS

| | Introduction | Pg 1 |

A BROKEN HEART

1	A Broken Heart	Pg 3
2	The Broken Heart Seeks Chaos	Pg 7
3	The Broken Heart Seeks Power	Pg 11
4	The Broken Heart is Proud	Pg 15
5	The Broken Heart Needs Affirmation	Pg 19
6	The Broken Heart Seeks Control	Pg 23

A MISGUIDED HEART

7	A Misguided Heart	Pg 27
8	The Misguided Heart is Insecure	Pg 31
9	The Misguided Heart is Greedy	Pg 35
10	The Misguided Heart Seeks False Security	Pg 39
11	The Misguided Heart Can't Admit Mistakes	Pg 43
12	The Misguided Heart Knows Best	Pg 47

CONTENTS

A COLD HEART

13	A Cold Heart	Pg 51
14	The Cold Heart is Bitter	Pg 55
15	The Cold Heart is Defensive	Pg 59
16	The Cold Heart is Dark	Pg 63
17	The Cold Heart is Fearful	Pg 67
18	The Cold Heart Denies Truth	Pg 71

A LONGING HEART

19	A Longing Heart	Pg 75
20	The Heart Longs to be Whole	Pg 79
21	The Heart Longs for Restoration	Pg 83
22	The Heart Longs for Fulfillment	Pg 87
23	The Heart Longs to Act	Pg 91
24	The Heart Longs for Life	Pg 95

A HEALED HEART

25	A Healed Heart	Pg 99
	Acknowledgments	Pg 103

Introduction

Well here we are, Christmas season. After a multi-year climb out of the pandemic, we are truly "back to normal" (whatever that means).

In my previous Christmas devotional from 2018, we looked at how crazy the Christmas season can be and ways in which we could reclaim the truth of God's plan for us despite the concerts and recitals, church obligations and giant family get-togethers – all while barely holding it together.

Who could imagine a Christmas where all of that would be wiped off the schedule? Who could believe the empty malls, the small (or non-existent) family gatherings, the completely free evenings in mid-December with no triple-booked Christmas events to attend? Who could predict waiting in drive-through pharmacy lines and high school parking lots to get tested because we ventured out to visit family? Or, even weirder, visiting with family through little boxes on a screen?

Covid quite literally changed everything, and yet here we

are, staring at our calendars for December and, if you are like me, wondering if we learned anything at all. Or are we back to where we were: stressed, frantic and exhausted?

The years of the pandemic forced us to ask some hard questions. My guess is you probably did make some changes, adjusting your way of viewing or doing things. I have friends who switched their kid's school, changed jobs, moved houses, or even moved to different states.

But, oh the heart… it's a tricky thing.

While the pandemic may have changed some things, it exacerbated others, including the state of our hearts. No vaccine can change our hearts. No lifting of emergency orders can lift the darkness out of our hearts. No world-altering event can actually alter the inclinations of our hearts.

Quite simply, our hearts are broken until we meet Jesus.

This Christmas we'll look at how the Bible is a story about God (not you). Which means it's a story about Jesus, and specifically it's about how He came to heal our broken, misguided, cold, and longing hearts.

In each section of this book (there are four) we'll focus on one of the main ways our hearts are broken by exploring three stories from the Old Testament and three from the New Testament. They'll reveal different variations of the same broken heart condition (insert any country western song about a broken heart). If you're the sort who skips to the back of the book to find out whodunit, let me spare you. Jesus is the answer to our broken hearts. What is so incredibly life-changing is that He has always been the answer to our broken hearts. 5,000 years ago, 2,000 years ago, and last week. Each day this month, we'll look at proof.

He's the answer in the summer and the winter, and most certainly during the month of December.

Thanks for reading; here we go!

Day 1
A Broken Heart

Each Christmas I set out my decorative Dickens' Home collection passed down to me from my mother. This is a source of much hilarity as I used to think they were ridiculous, and now I unabashedly put them up.

They're from the 1980s – some light bulbs don't work and replacements are hard to find. My Cratchit's Corner house has a missing signpost, and poor Tiny Tim's crutch is permanently broken so that Bob can never put him down. Also, I have a butler with no head carrying a tray of coffee around the village just, you know, headless.

My village is broken, and yet I put it up every year. I'm settling for my broken village, because it's better than no village at all.

We do the same thing with our hearts. They are broken, and we're settling for living with them because it's all we know. Plus, we don't think we can fix them. (Which is true, we can't.)

We may feel this, that our heart is broken, even when we are not sure what that means. Interestingly enough, both of the editors for this book, my dad and my friend Bryn, have pacemakers. Something (but not the same thing they'd both be quick to point out) about their physical hearts doesn't work quite right. We understand that.

But, at an emotional and spiritual level, what actually is it that's broken in our hearts, and what can be done about it? Is a broken village, a broken world, a broken heart, the best we can hope for? To answer that we have to go back to the beginning.

As in… "In the beginning God created the heavens and the earth." From Genesis 1:1, the first verse of the Bible.

You see, God designed us to be in relationship with Him in a perfect world, the Garden of Eden, where everything existed that our hearts needed to be whole. While the garden has often become just a terrible Sunday School flannel-graph or a cultural flashpoint in science debates, what happened there is actually fundamental to understanding our hearts this Christmas.

Sure, we don't fully know every detail. When did it happen? How do humans fit into the fossil record of other anthropoids? What about dinosaurs or the Big Bang?

I don't know; but I do know that God's design for us, as told in the story of creation, is true.

We can feel it. We can feel that we were made for a place where we are at peace with the world around us, ourselves, and with God. We were made for a world that God declared good. Animals and oceans, the sun and moon, men and women, trees and flowers (and I'm going to throw in pizza and hard cider) - all of it was created good. And yet, Adam and Eve ate the fruit.

> The serpent was the shrewdest of all the wild animals the Lord God had made. One day he asked the woman, "Did God really say you must not eat the fruit from any of the trees in the

> garden?"
>
> "Of course we may eat fruit from the trees in the garden," the woman replied. "It's only the fruit from the tree in the middle of the garden that we are not allowed to eat. God said, 'You must not eat it or even touch it; if you do, you will die.'"
>
> "You won't die!" the serpent replied to the woman. "God knows that your eyes will be opened as soon as you eat it, and you will be like God, knowing both good and evil."
>
> The woman was convinced. She saw that the tree was beautiful and its fruit looked delicious, and she wanted the wisdom it would give her. So she took some of the fruit and ate it. Then she gave some to her husband, who was with her, and he ate it, too. [Genesis 3:1-6]

You may wonder what the big deal is. They ate some fruit they weren't supposed to. So what? But it wasn't about the fruit. It was about a serpent whispering half truths and full lies, and about how they believed it. It was about them deciding they could have power with their shiny, new knowledge of good and evil. It was about, well... them.

But if you recall in my introduction, the Bible is all about God.

Adam and Eve chose to believe the lie, so instead of being allowed to stay in the garden and fill the earth the way God had designed them (and us) to do, they were exiled into a world that now included evil, and, more importantly, their hearts included it as well. So did the hearts of their children, and their children's children, all the way down to us.

And here we are this Christmas with broken hearts – hearts that know and often choose evil.

Our world will tell you that at your core you are a good person with perhaps bad circumstances. But it's the exact opposite. Our core, our hearts, are not good. When you believe the lie, you will be frustrated, confused, sad, angry and ultimately lost. You cannot find your way back to the garden, back to God's design for your heart, on your own. The world will say you can, and the world is lying to you. You are lying to yourself. We all do it, because that's what broken hearts do: they believe the lie, and then they spread the lie.

We can't fix what is broken, but God can.

This is the entire point of Christmas! Jesus came as an actual human baby while He was also fully God. He grew up and allowed His heart to break for us so that we could once again be in relationship with Him.

This Christmas Jesus offers to heal your broken heart and lead you back into the life you were meant for with true peace, real joy, and, someday, a return to a world where you fully belong. For the next few days, we'll look at ways in which a broken heart acts, and why the only real solution is to let Jesus heal it.

Let Jesus give you His heart that was fully broken for you, so yours can be fully healed in Him.

.

Day 2
The Broken Heart Seeks Chaos

A few years ago when our eldest daughter was entering middle school, we had a party for her class in our backyard. She decorated it with lights and glowing balloons and designed a crazy, fun obstacle course. It included running and crawling around the lawn with things such as cheese puffs, hula hoops, marshmallows, trash bags and shaving cream.

Our backyard was big, and it was hard to be at every obstacle station. My husband and I didn't quite notice the exact moment when things began to unravel that night. We only realized, as we marched up the hill to the finish line, that the station involving shaving cream had descended into that special chaos middle schoolers revel in.

Instead of a few discreet blobs of shaving cream on trash bags for the cheese puff toss, entire human beings (of the 14-year-old set) were covered head to toe in shaving cream. Hair was spiked with shaving cream. Faces were covered, eyes peering out into the darkness through shaving cream. The obstacle course had, in a word, devolved.

Having been teenagers once ourselves, my husband and I felt dumb that we hadn't foreseen this rather obvious outcome. If chaos is an option with teenagers, it will prevail.

Unfortunately, that's often how our hearts operate as well; and chaos is almost always an option. While the shaving cream chaos was fairly easy to clean up, the chaos of our hearts cannot be cleaned up with a few extra guest towels.

We see the chaos of brokenness way back in the story of Noah and the flood. It makes for a great children's story about animals and rainbows, and I will admit the Fisher Price Noah's Ark is nearly the perfect toy set (pssst, if you're looking for a last minute gift idea for a kid, this is a winner!). But just past the smiling hippos and snuggly matching giraffes is a dark story about what happens when our broken hearts veer into chaos.

The world grew bigger after Adam and Eve; there were more people and a growing culture, but it was going badly. In fact, we read in Genesis 6 that, "The Lord saw how great the wickedness of the human race had become on the earth, and that every inclination of the thoughts of the human heart was only evil all the time." [Genesis 6:5]

So God sent a flood to, in effect, wipe the slate clean. The consequence of the flood was that, "All were destroyed. The only people who survived were Noah and those with him in the boat." [Genesis 7:23]

It is a grim picture of how our broken hearts will function when chaos is an option.

But God didn't design our heart for chaos, and just as He provided a way through the flood for Noah and his family, He offers us a way out of the chaos as well. In fact, He promised a way. He told Noah that the rainbow was the sign of this promise. When we see a rainbow we are to remember there is a plan, there is hope, we will not live in a broken world with broken hearts forever.

Now, I'll have to ask that the cute children's books take a back seat, because do you know what a rainbow really is? Yes, yes, a prism and light refraction, but consider the shape. It's an arc, the arc of a bow. Not a bow like you might put on a Christmas present, but like a bow and arrow. The actual word for what we call a rainbow is the word for a bow in the original Hebrew language of the Old Testament. The ancient near eastern people didn't distinguish them as two different words, rather they saw rainbows as the weapons of the gods in heaven.

So when God told Noah, "I have set my bow in the cloud and it shall be a sign of the covenant between me and the earth" [Genesis 9:13], the actual words God used were those of a military leader, hanging up their weapon of war.

Was this because the flood washed away all the chaos and brokenness in the world and in our hearts? No. Clearly our hearts are still broken, unable to be in relationship with God like they were designed to be back in the garden. Rather, God was promising that He would provide the way to peace with Him – a way back. He was hanging up His weapon of war because His plan, and our hope, means peace with God. Not war. Not chaos. Not brokenness.

What we remember at Christmas is that Jesus came to let His own heart be broken, so that we could live at peace with Him. That's why Jesus can take your broken heart that is prone to chaos, and heal it. Christmas means an end to the chaos (maybe not an end to office parties, sorry). Christmas means the flood cannot reach you if you let Jesus heal your broken heart.

Let Jesus give you His heart that was fully broken for you, so yours can be fully healed in Him.

Day 3
The Broken Heart Seeks Power

Now that I've written three books, it's time to let you in on a secret. I'm actually famous. When I was a freshman in college I was on the Oprah show. I know, I know. It's hard to believe you've been reading devotionals from such a well-known person all these years, but it's true.

Okay, so it wasn't a Tom-Cruise-on-the-couch Oprah appearance, and I'm not sure it's made any of the top ten Oprah interview moments. But for about thirty seconds in 1993, I was hauled out of my audience seat by Oprah (her show taped in Chicago, where I lived at the time, and it was easy to get tickets during her early career) and asked to recount my riveting experience with credit card fraud.

When the episode aired, both my future mother-in-law prepping dinner in her kitchen in Philadelphia and a high school friend shopping in Sears saw me on TV. Me! In an olive green blazer with shoulder pads and hair that looked like a mushroom cloud.

(I'll be doing autographs later on if you're interested.)

It's possible I was only famous in my mind; but I couldn't

believe I'd managed to speak on a national TV show and that people had seen me states away. I was thrilled and it's become part of my "Two Truths and a Lie" repertoire.

Fame, and having people notice you, is enticing and can be fun. It often seems like it will make a lot of things better. We associate famous people with power and status, and with those things, we believe, comes security. Our broken hearts crave that because we keep believing that we can handle everything ourselves. That was the lie that was whispered in the garden, and that whisper continued even after the flood. It traveled into the new people groups that grew up out of Noah's family, and they expanded until there were enough people to have a city. With a city the people desired power, and fame, and ultimately what they believed to be security.

They said, "Come, let's make bricks… let's build a great city for ourselves with a tower that reaches into the sky. This will make us famous and keep us from being scattered all over the world." [Genesis 11:4]

You may know what happened. (Though, interestingly, there is not a Fisher Price set for the Tower of Babel.) What happened is that God came down. Turns out their big tower didn't quite reach high enough to get to God. Maybe not enough bricks? He saw that they were trying to be famous, to be known, to achieve a level of power and status, to be safe all on their own, apart from Him.

That never goes well.

God scattered them and sent them all over the earth (which had been His original command to Noah after the flood anyway) and gave them multiple languages so that they wouldn't try the whole tower thing again… at least for a while.

Because here we are now. The Tower of Babel happened before recorded history, basically a really, really long time ago; but our broken hearts still think that if we can make a name for ourselves, if we can just get enough power and prestige, we'll be secure. We'll have it made. We'll build our own tower with bricks made of a great education, fancy homes, really successful kids or money. We believe the lie that this will make us safe.

Our hearts will always crave power, and if we listen to the lie we'll crave the wrong sort of power. Face it, our broken hearts don't know anything else.

But God doesn't look down on our power hungry little piles of bricks and scatter us like He did with the people in Genesis. Instead, He sent Jesus down to us. And Jesus, through His saving work, gives us His renown, His success, and His safety. It's not a renown and success like the world chases, and it certainly is not like a fleeting cameo on an Oprah show. No, what Jesus offers is so much more, and it's the only security and the only name we'll ever need.

This Christmas Jesus offers us His heart and His name. His success didn't really do much by the world's standards. He had a short three year ministry and seemingly failed when He was killed on a cross. But by God's eternal standards, by the only standards that matter, His success over death itself through the resurrection is the greatest power, the greatest security, that has ever existed or ever will. And He offers that to you if you let Him heal your broken heart.

Let Jesus give you His heart that was fully broken for you, so yours can be fully healed in Him.

Day 4
The Broken Heart is Proud

I often feel the need to break into song. A word or phrase will remind me of some lyrics, or a situation will occur that begs a certain musical interpretation layered into it. This is of course mostly done around my two teenage daughters. One is totally unfazed, and one whips out her ever present emotional shovel and digs a hole to the very core of the earth where she hides from her off-tune mother. That in turn only makes me sing more; in fact I'll probably begin to sing the lyrics from the song "40" by U2: "How long to sing this song? How long, how long, ho-ow looooooonggg, how long."

Not only that, but I am told I talk too loudly and everyone in the store/restaurant/school/church does not need to hear everything I say. To which I reply, "WHAT? I CAN'T HEAR YOU."

Parenting is fun.

But not all loud talkers and singers are there merely to embarrass their children, and sometimes drawing attention to oneself is a sign of a broken heart – a sign of a heart that seeks to put itself near the top, at the expense of others. A heart that puts others down in order to feel important.

Jesus told a story about this very sort of person in one of His parables.

> Two men went to the Temple to pray. One was a Pharisee, and the other was a despised tax collector. The Pharisee stood by himself and prayed this prayer: "I thank you, God, that I am not like other people – cheaters, sinners, adulterers. I'm certainly not like that tax collector! I fast twice a week, and I give you a tenth of my income." But the tax collector stood at a distance and dared not even lift his eyes to heaven as he prayed. Instead, he beat his chest in sorrow, saying, "O God, be merciful to me, for I am a sinner." I tell you, this sinner, not the Pharisee, returned home justified before God. For those who exalt themselves will be humbled, and those who humble themselves will be exalted. [Luke 18:10-14]

The Pharisee wanted to get God's attention; he wanted to look important and showcase all of his fabulous qualities. He wanted to be admired and praised. He wanted glory. But Jesus said his big, fancy, loud, very public prayer was pointless. Why? Well, because his heart was broken. He only felt good enough by making the tax collector look bad. His misplaced pride was his downfall.

It's an easy trap to fall into, perhaps especially this time of year. How often do we let our broken hearts put others down so we can grab a moment of fleeting pride or a feeling of smugness that we are better? How often do we make slight comments or insinuations trying to put ourselves in a better standing with a coworker, a friend group, or, dare I say, a Bible study?

What our hearts really want is what Jesus says the tax collector received: to be "justified before God." Justified is a theological term that means being in good or right standing with God. Remember that's what we were designed for way back in the garden, to be in a relationship with God, to be right with Him.

When Jesus saw the tax collector, He saw a man who was justified and accepted by God. But he was a tax collector, a social pariah! How could that be?

In case you think you'd handle it better than the Pharisee did, ask yourself who you would look down on if they walked into your office, or your church, or your school. You know, one of "those" people, people, if we are honest, we think we are better than.

The truth is, none of us live up to God's standard, and the tax collector knew that. He knew he didn't deserve God, and yet God was the only One who could save him from his broken heart.

This Christmas the stress may push you to the edge, and you may want to snap out at people who aren't living up to your standards. You may want to put others down to make yourself feel better. You may know you are "too loud," but feel incapable of acting any other way. Good news: Jesus came for people just like that! Some of Jesus' disciples were ex-Pharisees and former know-it-alls. He can take your loud, brash, broken heart and give you His. His heart will give you what you actually long for: to be in good standing with God.

Let Jesus give you His heart that was fully broken for you, so yours can be fully healed in Him.

Day 5
The Broken Heart Needs Affirmation

Christmas can exacerbate the best and the worst in our personalities. We can become more joyful and generous, but also more, well, insane. One of the many traps I fall into is becoming too much of a people pleaser. I hate to say "no" at Christmas. I over schedule, overbuy, overcommit and overthink everything. I feel frantic much of the season trying to make sure everyone is getting a present that is exciting and splashy but also thoughtful, creative, and personal. I want the gifts I give to be so much more than just a gift. It's ridiculous. I know that as I type this; I also know around late October I'll begin to dither over catalogs selling customized cheese boards and monogrammed slippers and penknives that turn into telescopes.

Of course, I know that's not the real point of Christmas, and I've been at this long enough that I can sometimes snap myself out of it and refocus. But it's hard. When the season gets louder, the music is jingling and the crowds begin to gather, I feel my own inclination to try and meet all of the demands.

This is a symptom of a broken heart. A broken heart wants approval and affirmation from the people around it. A broken heart needs the praise of people, no matter how wrong the request is.

Pontius Pilate was one such man with a broken heart. He met and interviewed Jesus, and found Him innocent. But the screaming crowds had gathered outside, and as the yelling grew louder, his political career began to teeter on the edge. He wanted to make all the angry, crazy people happy. Pilate heard Jesus proclaim His innocence, and he knew it to be true.

> "Are you the king of the Jews?" he [Pilate] asked Him.
>
> Jesus replied, "Is this your own question, or did others tell you about me?"
>
> "Am I a Jew?" Pilate retorted. "Your own people and their leading priests brought you to me for trial. Why? What have you done?"
>
> Jesus answered, "My Kingdom is not an earthly kingdom. If it were, my followers would fight to keep me from being handed over to the Jewish leaders. But my Kingdom is not of this world."
>
> Pilate said, "So you are a king?"
>
> Jesus responded, "You say I am a king. Actually, I was born and came into the world to testify to the truth. All who love the truth recognize that what I say is true."
>
> "What is truth?" Pilate asked. Then he went out again to the people and told them, "He is not guilty of any crime." [John 18:33-38]

Even though Pilate didn't find Jesus guilty, he wanted to

make the people happy. He played the "your truth is not my truth" card with Jesus. He wanted to pretend to believe the truth that the people claimed, not the truth, the actual source of all truth – Truth with a capital T – who stood right in front of him. So he knowingly sent an innocent man, Jesus, off to be crucified.

We do the same thing with our broken hearts. We want to make people happy; we allow their truth to be our truth, even when secretly we disagree. We give into the lie that somehow this will make things better. Their fake truth, their affirmation, their happiness outweighs what we know to be true and real. Over time, like the lie whispered in the garden, we even start to believe it. But believing a lie will never really please anyone, and it will always hurt our hearts and the hearts of others.

The only person who we really need to please is Jesus, and here's the thing: we can't please Him on our own. We can only please Him when we let Him give us His heart, and His truth, the real truth. This truth states that we are broken people in need of new hearts, in need of saving, in need of a restored relationship with God. God's approval is the only approval that truly matters.

It can be very hard to let go of this aspect of our broken hearts. Especially this time of year; the approval of others has so much power over us.

But Jesus has more power.

If you let your heart rest in His approval, based on His life, then you will never need to listen to the chaos of the crowd again. You can live in the truth and approval of Jesus.

Let Jesus give you His heart that was fully broken for you, so yours can be fully healed in Him.

Day 6
The Broken Heart Seeks Control

It's not really a Christian devotional book unless I cite some Lord of the Rings, by J. R. R. Tolkien. If you've been in church-land long enough, you'll know that. If you are new to church-land, let's just say you have escaped some really long (and possibly overwrought) sermon illustrations.

But the story of the Hobbits and their journey to destroy a ring does have its illustrative merits. For example, the ring controls whoever wears it, and ultimately it gives power to that person to control others. The ring inscription even says, "One ring to rule them all, one ring to find them, one ring to bring them all and in the darkness bind them."

Fun, eh?

It doesn't sound too great. Yet what if you could find such a ring and have total control? What if you could snap your fingers and fix people, jobs, things? What if you could have everything you needed to succeed in this world?

It's a story that goes all the way back to the lie in the garden, and it's a story that keeps finding new ways of offering a bright, shiny ring that, maybe, we should reach out and touch. Maybe we could carry it and not get corrupted? Maybe, just once?

This story, this whisper, this lie about ultimate control carries through the Bible, including in the New Testament story of Ananias and Sapphira in the earliest days of the church in the book of Acts. The new Christians, the new followers of Jesus, were sharing things and working together to build a community. They often brought things they owned such as food or deeds to land to give to the church in order to help others in need. Ananias and Sapphira wanted in on the action, but their story took a sharp turn:

> There was a certain man named Ananias who, with his wife, Sapphira, sold some property. He brought part of the money to the apostles, claiming it was the full amount. With his wife's consent, he kept the rest. Then Peter said, "Ananias, why have you let Satan fill your heart? You lied to the Holy Spirit, and you kept some of the money for yourself. The property was yours to sell or not sell, as you wished. And after selling it, the money was also yours to give away. How could you do a thing like this? You weren't lying to us but to God!" When Ananias heard this, he fell down and died. [Acts 5:1-5]

Community living was all well and good, but they wanted a backup plan. When Sapphira came to Peter to check on the deal that Ananias made, she lied about the full sale too, and she also fell over dead.

It wasn't that they kept some of the money (Peter never asked them for the full amount); it's that they lied about it. They devised a way to look good but still keep a bit of control over their lives in case the whole "early church thing" didn't quite pan out. They were unwilling to truly be part of the community in spirit. Instead, they secretly tried to retain control… just in case.

Just in case turned into just plain dead. Peter was quite clear it was because they tried to manipulate the situation – attempting to retain control while acting like they weren't. They tried to rule it all.

It's the condition of our hearts to want to rule it all, to seek control. Being in control feels like a good way to make sure our hearts won't get broken again.

But the Bible says there is only one God, and, as one of my former pastors, Pastor Ray, often says, "He's God, and you're not." You aren't in control of, quite frankly, anything. Not your job, not your house, not your kids, or, much of the time, your feelings. You can't power-play your way to an unbroken heart. There is only one way to fix the power struggle, and that is to admit that Jesus is the King and you are a subject in His glorious kingdom.

Let your broken heart rest, truly rest, knowing that Jesus is in control, sitting on the throne. Let your heart say, as Paul says in 1 Corinthians 8:6, "There is but one God, the Father, from whom all things came and for whom we exist. And there is but one Lord, Jesus Christ, through whom all things came and through whom we exist."

Rather than a ring that binds us in the darkness, Jesus has the power to bind us all in His marvelous light.

Let Jesus give you His heart that was fully broken for you, so yours can be fully healed in Him.

Day 7
A Misguided Heart

The first year our eldest, very tall daughter played basketball, she loved it, but she was just learning. More importantly, I was new to it and didn't really know what was going on. So when she got the ball and headed towards the basket, pulling away from the pack of girls, I was happy I knew what to do. I jumped to my feet and I screamed and cheered and generally went wild. She had the ball! Already in her first game! It was magical! I believed in her, she believed in her, it was thrilling.

It was the wrong basket.

No matter how much we believed that she was doing the right thing, no matter how much maternal love I poured into my enthusiastic cheering and jumping, no matter how great and exciting and incredible it felt – it was still wrong. We couldn't will it to be the right basket. It just wasn't.

That's how our hearts are now. No matter how much we want to do the right thing, or go in the right direction, or make the right choice. We just can't. The fancy theological term for this is "total depravity," and it means even our best work, our kindest acts, our most selfless moments, apart from Jesus, are tainted by that very first heartbreak back in the garden. We can't choose correctly anymore on our own, and even when it is close, it's still not close enough.

Our hearts are lost. If given the directions, we can't follow them. If told to make the basket, we'll run the wrong way. Our hearts lead us astray, despite how much we believe we may be going in the right direction. We feel this in little and big ways every day.

We can't will ourselves, on our own, to set our hearts in the right direction.

The book of Proverbs in the Old Testament is a series of sayings and words of wisdom that were mostly written by King Solomon, son of King David. Proverbs 3:1-6 has a lot to say about how we can make sure we're going in the right direction. (Spoiler alert: it's not because we can do it alone.)

> My child, never forget the things I have taught you.
> Store my commands in your heart
> If you do this, you will live many years,
> and your life will be satisfying.
> Never let loyalty and kindness leave you!
> Tie them around your neck as a reminder.
> Write them deep within your heart. T
> hen you will find favor with both God and people,
> and you will earn a good reputation.
> Trust in the Lord with all your heart;
> do not depend on your own understanding.
> Seek His will in all you do,
> and He will show you which path to take.
> [Proverbs 3:1-6]

Do you see the three times the heart is mentioned? Each time it's in relationship to obeying God's commandments, which is another way of saying that God's directions are the only ones to follow. It's not about our own great ideas or self-help programs; it's not about digging deep enough to find the inner good that we wish flickered in our hearts. No. It's about having God in our heart and, therefore, His commandments, His love, His faithfulness – not ours.

Do you want to walk in the right direction? Do you want to have a heart that guides you in the right way? Let God direct it; that is how our paths will be made straight. Not from our own understanding, but from God's.

This is not popular in our culture, especially at Christmas with a commercialized version of kindness and inner peace. The commercialized, candy-cane-latte-Christmas preaches that spending will promote harmony and joy, magically making us the good, warm, fuzzy people we would like to be. Our culture tells us to find the wisdom that is in us, to trust our instincts and to listen to our hearts.

But it's just the opposite. We spent the last section looking at how our hearts are broken, and one of the very real side effects of that is that we are lost. Our broken heart may get us to the mall to buy a really great present, but it won't direct us to true peace or real joy. And isn't that what we really want (and want to give) this Christmas?

This year you don't have to be lost. God can direct your paths and give you all that you need to know to live and choose well. For the next few days, we'll look at ways a misguided heart can lead us astray, and why the only true solution is to let Jesus give us His heart and His understanding so that He can make our paths straight.

Let Jesus give you His heart that was fully broken for you, so yours can be fully healed in Him.

Day 8
The Misguided Heart Blames Others

For a few years my husband and I lived in the city of Chicago. We commuted to corporate jobs in "the Loop" on the "El" to our offices (cubicles) in skyscrapers in the bustling, busy city. It was eye-opening and new to me, given my ministry-based background. So when I was asked to join an international call with our Australian team, I was thrilled. It felt exotic, and I was proud to be invited. Even though the call was at 3 a.m.

This was before Zoom or cell phones were a part of life, so it meant that I had to set up a corded phone in the spare bedroom of our apartment and sneak out at the right time so as to not wake my husband.

That early morning I shuffled into our guest room and dialed in, tented beneath the spare bedroom covers. Suddenly I felt a *whack!* It was Panguar Ban, our cat.

Whack! Whack!

I could feel him batting me as I kept up my professional tone. Batting, or was it pouncing? And then I saw it, and I screamed. There was a mouse running across me, followed by the cat, followed by me levitating bodily up and out of the room, phone attached by the cord in hand. I landed in our living room, slamming the guest room door behind me.

There was a pause on the call.

"Oi, everything ok, Esther?" the partner asked in her Australian accent. (Fine, maybe she didn't say "Oi," but then again, maybe she did.)

"Oh, yes, sorry. Just, um, my cat."

But I was embarrassed and upset. I had wanted to impress them on my first international call. Instead, I had screamed into the phone like a wild person – a person who had a mouse in her guest room.

With my pent up emotion, I called our landlord later that day to let her know how unacceptable it was. I demanded she hire an exterminator and deal with the "mouse problem."

"Oh, ok sure. I'll get right on that," she replied as if I had lost my actual mind.

It was a ridiculous demand. We lived in a city apartment near restaurants and venues of all kinds. She explained to me that our building did have a standard exterminator contract, but city living meant the occasional mouse got in.

I'd misplaced my embarrassment and anger onto her, when really it belonged on me.

Misguided hearts will often place embarrassment and anger onto others. Our misguided hearts seek to deflect the fault of failing from where it belongs – squarely on us.

This happened in the Old Testament story of Joseph. His father, Isaac, clearly favored him. When Joseph began to have dreams about his future greatness, his brothers (all eleven of them) were angry. They weren't the favorites. They didn't have special dreams. They were jealous, and they blamed Joseph. So when an opportunity arose, they sold him to slavers headed to Egypt, and they assumed they'd never hear from him again. They even told their father that Joseph was dead.

But if you know the story, you know that God took this evil situation that Joseph's brothers created and transformed it into the way Joseph ultimately would save his brothers, and all of his family, from famine. After being sold into slavery, Joseph rose to prominence in Pharaoh's kingdom and ultimately became the leader in charge of managing food resources. The brothers, seeking food for their families back in Israel, traveled to Egypt where they encountered this powerful Egyptian leader. When Joseph finally told his brothers who he was, he explained this to them:

> Then Joseph said to his brothers, "Come close to me." When they had done so, he said, "I am your brother Joseph, the one you sold into Egypt! And now, do not be distressed and do not be angry with yourselves for selling me here, because it was to save lives that God sent me ahead of you. For two years now there has been famine in the land, and for the next five years there will be no plowing and reaping. But God sent me ahead of you to preserve for you a remnant on earth and to save your lives by a great deliverance." [Genesis 45:4-7]

The brothers' hearts were misguided. What they did was wrong, hurtful and deadly. They allowed their jealous anger to guide them down a path that would have led to death.

The same misguided, broken thinking is true for us, too, and it may be more enticing or tempting this time of year, when tempers are short and the pace is frenetic. It's so easy to let our embarrassment, anger or version of what we think "should have happened" control us. When we blame others instead of ourselves, we will go down the wrong path. Our misguided hearts will live in the land of famine forever, unless God invites us to the land of plenty.

Which He does. Jesus invites us out of our lost and misguided ways, out of our attempts to blame others for our anger and embarrassment when life doesn't work out (pssst it never works out), into His land of plenty.

Let Jesus give you His heart that was fully broken for you, so yours can be fully healed in Him.

Day 9
The Misguided Heart is Greedy

I've been all types of sports mom over the years, but these days I'm primarily a volleyball mom to my high school junior. It's lots of miles, lots of warehouses, lots of cold bleachers and lots (too many!?) of whistles. And peppered in there amongst the first aid stand and referee's table is the glint of lots of medals.

Medaling at a tournament is a hotly debated topic in terms of who qualifies, which tier, and what level; but everyone agrees that if your kid gets one it's a big deal. So when our daughter's club team won their first medal, it felt great. They'd come in second after five weekends of tournaments. Slogging their way ever closer, set by set, match by match, until finally they came out at the top. A silver medal, after all that work, was exciting, rewarding and… sparkly. It was a big old shiny thing that hung around their necks showing them off for the champions they were.

But it wasn't gold.

As the team walked by that did receive the gold, it was hard not to feel… something. It had been a fair match, but there was a brief moment where I felt resentful. I wanted my daughter to get a gold medal even if her team hadn't won it. We deserved the silver, but I wanted more.

Her silver medal hangs in her closet now – out of sight except when it bangs against the door (which happens every single time she opens or closes it, ask me how I know). It's a fun memory from many months ago because, as I write this, the next season is upon us. I can't wait to get back to it, except… I remember that feeling of wanting more than I had.

Wanting what we don't have is so much a part of our broken hearts, especially this time of year. When we are misguided, we become greedy. We think a sparkly, shiny thing – a job, degree, relationship, trip, bank account, or just something we saw on Amazon – will give us what we most need. Plus, we want it.

We see this in the story of Achan found in the Old Testament book of Joshua. God commanded the Israelites not to keep any of the plunder from the battles they fought as they began to live in the promised land. They were to rely on God alone to provide. They were not to get tangled up by the cultures around them. That meant not keeping their idols, their clothes, their household items, their food, nothing. God commanded them to either destroy it or set it aside as an offering to Him.

But Achan wanted more. His heart wasn't satisfied and he didn't trust God to give him what was best. He saw things that seemed better than what he had, and he wanted them. In the next battle, they lost; and God told their leader, Joshua, that it was because someone, somewhere, in the Israelite's camp had taken the plunder. After a long search they finally came to Achan.

> Then Joshua said to Achan, "My son, give glory to the Lord, the God of Israel, by telling the

> truth. Make your confession and tell me what you have done. Don't hide it from me." Achan replied, "It is true! I have sinned against the Lord, the God of Israel. Among the plunder I saw a beautiful robe from Babylon, 200 silver coins, and a bar of gold weighing more than a pound. I wanted them so much that I took them. They are hidden in the ground beneath my tent, with the silver buried deeper than the rest." [Joshua 7:19-21]

Achan saw the glint of gold, and he wanted it. The gold was meant to be dedicated to God, and he took it instead. But the silver, a robe, and a shiny bar of gold couldn't give Achan what his heart really wanted, and his greed ultimately led to his death.

Christmas is certainly a time where material things can catch our eyes. Even non-material things seem to loom a little larger. It's easy to want the next thing, the sparkly thing, the gold; but it won't satisfy.

Even when our greedy hearts get what they want, like Achan did, it's not enough. There is no bar (or medal) of gold that can truly satisfy our hearts. When we allow ourselves to follow that desire, we will be going in the wrong direction. What our hearts truly need is Jesus. The heart of Jesus Himself is far better than any gold or job or title, and He offers it to you. His heart will provide the satisfaction you truly desire.

Let Jesus give you His heart that was fully broken for you, so yours can be fully healed in Him.

Day 10
The Misguided Heart Relies on False Security

"Fire!" I yelled. And then again, "GET UP! FIRE!"

It was around 11 p.m., and I woke up in our Chicago apartment to a funny flickering light. When I raised my head and looked out our window, I was stunned to see the entire building behind us going up in flames. This was the city; if the building behind us was on fire, there was a decent chance our building would be on fire soon as well.

I have an "instant-on" crisis mode, and by the time my husband woke up and realized he needed to get dressed, I'd already thrown on jeans, grabbed two pieces of jewelry that had sentimental value, our paper airplane tickets (remember when you got paper plane tickets in the mail?) for an upcoming trip, and Panguar Ban (the cat from Day 8). I threw the cat into his cat carrier, and the tickets and jewelry in behind him, and we left.

From the sidewalk, we watched the flames grow higher and begin to jump the alley. The siding on our apartment melted, the back bumper of our car melted, and our trash cans oozed into plastic blobs.

In the end, our apartment, smoky and smelly, stayed standing, while our neighbors lost everything (though they themselves were unharmed). It was a weird, scary, sad feeling.

On the one hand, we had no kids and no possessions of value that couldn't get thrown into a cat carrier. On the other hand, it was unnerving to realize that in an instant, all the things that we owned and had moved three times at that point – things that seemed such a permanent part of our lives, like our ugly couch, our IKEA furniture, our hand-me down desks – could have gone up in smoke if the wind had shifted just slightly.

Our hearts are often like that. We allow ourselves to be lulled into a false sense of security because we have things that seem so stable. We find security in tangible things like houses, apartments, or cars, but also through intangible things such as our jobs, our degrees, our health, our friendships, and even our families. We treat these things as if they are permanent because they give us a sense of security and comfort.

But they don't all last, and they aren't permanent.

There was a rich young man in the New Testament who learned this after talking to Jesus. He asked Him how he could be saved, and the conversation went as follows:

> Jesus replied: "You must not murder. You must not commit adultery. You must not steal. You must not testify falsely. Honor your father and mother. Love your neighbor as yourself."
>
> "I've obeyed all these commandments," the young man replied. "What else must I do?"
>
> Jesus told him, "If you want to be perfect, go and sell all your possessions and give the money to the poor, and you will have treasure in

heaven. Then come, follow me."

But when the young man heard this, he went away sad, for he had many possessions. [Matthew 19:18-22]

Why couldn't the man do that? Didn't he know how to sell things on eBay? No. He thought he could keep his heart safe based on the things of this world. His things were his security; but Jesus was asking him to trust his heart to a world Jesus offered, a world where Jesus would provide the security.

We're no different than the young man; it's an easy trap to fall into. The misguided heart confuses the temporary security of this world with the eternal security that comes from following Jesus.

This man followed his heart – his sad, misguided heart. But we don't have to. This Christmas our culture is going to make a lot of fuss about things. About stuff you can touch and wrap and hold, about things you can do to stand out and gain status. The big cars with the bows in the snowy driveway. The perfect Oprah sweater. The beauty products that keep selling out but promise to finally make you look younger. It will be easy for you to believe these things will provide you with real security. I know, because it's easy for me (ask me about my under-eye cream collection).

Don't let your heart be fooled. Jesus offers the same thing to you as He did to the man in the passage. This Christmas, you do not have to go away sad like the rich young man. Instead, you can find absolute security and certainty about your life now and forever by following Jesus. Let Jesus give you true security.

Let Jesus give you His heart that was fully broken for you, so yours can be fully healed in Him.

Day 11
The Misguided Heart Can't Admit Mistakes

I'm not a big brand person, but for some reason this one brand of casual shoes caught my attention a few years ago as being stylish, comfortable, and extremely durable. My feet get trampled by our giant dogs on an hourly basis, so durability and comfort matter; being fashionable is just icing on the cake – a cake I rarely partake in. As a result, I sort of went crazy. I bought pairs in a variety of colors and styles and put them on my birthday and Christmas lists. I'm wearing a pair right now as I type this. They're turquoise.

But I didn't have a black pair, and who doesn't have black? It's a staple. So when I saw the online ad for 40% off I was thrilled. Within about five minutes I had a black pair, for almost half the price, whizzing my way.

Except they were whizzing from China, not California where my other shoes had come from. Even odder, when they arrived they were packed in Chinese newspaper and missing the signature branded blue stripe down the back. Also, some hot glue was hanging off the side of one shoe.

It was obvious. I'd been scammed.

After being a big mouth about not getting scammed to my daughters, I was now forced to accept that it was easier than it seemed. I also was forced to wear my fake, black shoes because I was not about to admit defeat. They weren't as comfortable or durable and the string of hot glue took the luster off the style part. They were fake, uncomfortable, evidence of my poor judgment, and I was stuck with them.

Our misguided hearts do dumb, sometimes truly hurtful and bad things; but it is when we refuse to admit that we messed up that we can get stuck.

This is illustrated in the story we find in Luke 7 when Jesus was invited to eat at the home of a Pharisee named Simon. Simon clearly thought he had it all together. He was educated, a religious leader, and had the famous teacher, Jesus, eating in his home. When a woman who had a bad reputation came into his house and used a very expensive bottle of perfume to wash, or anoint, Jesus' feet, Simon got his nose out of joint. He was offended that this low-level nobody would dare to presume to interact with, let alone anoint, Jesus.

But Jesus called him out for thinking he was any better.

> "Look at this woman kneeling here. When I entered your home, you didn't offer me water to wash the dust from my feet, but she has washed them with her tears and wiped them with her hair. You didn't greet me with a kiss, but from the time I first came in, she has not stopped kissing my feet. You neglected the courtesy of olive oil to anoint my head, but she has anointed my feet with rare perfume. I tell you, her sins – and they are many – have been forgiven, so she has shown me much love. But a person who is forgiven little shows only little love." [Luke 7:44-47]

The irony was, of course, that Jesus was teaching that the person who had the most to forgive was the one who was most grateful. Simon had just as much sin in his heart as the woman, but he kept telling himself that he was just fine. We all do. Our hearts are all broken beyond our ability to repair; it's just some of us try to hide it.

Simon was left to look foolish and ungrateful in his own home. His misguided heart caused him to think he could hide his sins, perhaps distracting Jesus by his fancy degree and nice house.

Home, jobs, fancy titles, cute shoes... Jesus doesn't care. Jesus wants our hearts. The heart of the sinful woman was one of sorrow for her sins and gratitude to even have the chance to meet Jesus and offer Him hospitality.

This Christmas you may need to admit you made mistakes, you may need to ask for help, you may need to acknowledge that Jesus guides us along the only path that matters, a path that has nothing to do with our great choices. The woman knew that; she put herself at the feet of Jesus, and He gave her His heart. If we follow our misguided hearts, we are likely to find ourselves well-dressed, but alone. Let Jesus be the reason you feel confident, chosen, and loved this Christmas. He sees who you really are, and calls you to Him anyway.

Let Jesus give you His heart that was fully broken for you, so yours can be fully healed in Him.

Day 12
The Misguided Heart Thinks it Knows Best

A few years back, our family took a vacation to Hawaii to the island of Maui. On a previous visit, we'd driven the famous Road to Hana, a scenic drive around the northeast corner of the island. Further, we'd taken a loose interpretation of our rental car's policy about off-roading and had also driven all the way around the southeastern side. It had some rough roads, but nothing we couldn't handle. This time, filled with confidence that we understood the road warnings, we planned to drive the final stretch around the northwest corner. How hard could it be? We rented a giant SUV, based on our previous experience, and set off.

Only, the sort of car you need to make tight hairpin turns is actually the opposite of a giant SUV. There were turns where the hood of our car looked larger than the width of the road, giving the appearance (which I chose to believe was my reality) of the car dangling out into space above the ocean before crashing into rocks far below.

I have never been so terrified. The problem was, we couldn't turn around. Our car was so big, and the roads were so narrow, there was nothing to do but go forward. It was a horrifying drive; yet we just kept going forward.

We've talked a lot about the various ways our hearts are misguided this week, and how that ultimately means we think we know best.

Jesus tells a fairly well-known story about a prodigal son who thought he knew best as well. It's actually a story about two sons who both went down the wrong paths – two different paths, both wrong. Both sons were unable to redirect themselves without their father's help. The younger son took all his inheritance money, rebelled against his father, and went off to live the "good life." When the good life got bad, he dug in. He kept digging until he lost all his money and was living with pigs. Only then did he finally admit he needed help and decided to go back to his father. Not as his son, but as a servant.

Meanwhile, the older son didn't make any mistakes at all, and let everyone know how amazing he was. He'd never left his father and never squandered a dime. In case you missed it, he was super incredible. When the younger brother came crawling back for help, the older brother wanted to show him no mercy or grace. After all, he'd never had any problems and didn't see why his brother deserved a break.

But their father threw a party for the younger brother, and reminded the older brother he already had all that he needed.

> Look, dear son, you have always stayed by me, and everything I have is yours. We had to celebrate this happy day. For your brother was dead and has come back to life! He was lost, but now he is found! [Luke 15:31-32]

The younger brother had gone to the very end of a dark and wrong path, and yet the love of his father changed his heart and life. We don't know about the older one. The story ends there. It's quite possible that, like so many of us, he let his misguided heart keep leading him down a path of legalism, bitterness, and anger, believing he was perfect. Perfectly miserable and misguided.

Perhaps this Christmas you are chasing things you think will make you happy, running as fast as you can for what looks like success or happiness while falling deeper and deeper into a world that will never satisfy. Or perhaps you are judging others for being so difficult and challenging during this season and feeling smug that you aren't like them. Or maybe you're a little of both brothers – scared, sad and slightly panicked about life, yet slapping on a fake smile and doing the next amazing, perfect thing.

Either way your heart is misguided; it's lost. You're way far down the wrong path. But Jesus loves us and wants us to follow Him on the right path. If you follow Him, what is His is yours this Christmas. We don't have to keep going down the wrong path. The Father is waiting! He is ready to run to you and bring you back to safety. In fact, He'll throw you a party! A real Christmas party that is bigger and better than any party you can imagine.

Let Jesus heal your misguided heart. Let Him find you out there where you are lost and declare you found, putting you on His road, the only road that is going the right direction.

Let Jesus give you His heart that was fully broken for you, so yours can be fully healed in Him.

Day 13
A Cold Heart

There are a few well-known Christmas stories that are part of our cultural fabric and, interestingly, two of the most familiar have characters with the same central flaw. In one we find Ebenezer Scrooge, Dickens' loved-to-be-hated character who didn't care about anyone other than his miserly, nasty self.

> He carried his own low temperature always about with him; he iced his office in the dog-days, and didn't thaw it one degree at Christmas. External heat and cold had little influence on Scrooge. No warmth could warm, nor wintry weather chill him.
> [*A Christmas Carol*, Charles Dickens]

He was a cold, loathsome man. Very much like our other famous Christmas icon from the annals of high literature: the Grinch.

> The Grinch hated Christmas!
> The whole Christmas season!
> Now, please don't ask why.
> No one quite knows the reason.
> It could be his head wasn't screwed on just right.
> It could be, perhaps his shoes were too tight.
> But I think that the most likely reason of all
> May have been that his heart
> was two sizes too small.
> [*How the Grinch Stole Christmas*, Dr. Seuss]

Scrooge and the Grinch. Both had a heart problem. Their hearts were cold and small; and we know that once a heart is cold, it's actually dead.

Perhaps at Christmas we sense even more than normal that we also have a heart problem. We feel our cold, small hearts, but there is nothing we can do about it. We can't revive ourselves.

Ezekiel shows us this picture in the Old Testament. He talks about us having hearts of stone, and he talks about people as bones lying in a valley. Lifeless, no pulse, no beating heart. Just a heap of bones. I referenced this image in my last Christmas devotional because it's just the perfect image of what our reality is, whether we admit it or not.

Ezekiel was talking to the Israelites in chapters 36 and 37 of the book named for him, but also to all of us who try to fix our own heart problems. It never works. In the end, we end up broken and dead. But God can, and does, revive our cold, dead hearts. God said:

> I will sprinkle clean water on you, and you will be clean; I will cleanse you from all your impurities and from all your idols. I will give you a new heart and put a new spirit in you; I

> will remove from you your heart of stone and give you a heart of flesh. [Ezekiel 36:25-26]

Then He said:

> Prophesy to these bones and say to them, "Dry bones, hear the word of the Lord! This is what the Sovereign Lord says to these bones: I will make breath enter you, and you will come to life. I will attach tendons to you and make flesh come upon you and cover you with skin; I will put breath in you, and you will come to life. Then you will know that I am the Lord." [Ezekiel 37:4-5]

Warm beating hearts of flesh instead of cold hearts of stone. Bones with tendons and skin and life. This is what God does for us. We are in the valley of dry bones. Our hearts are lifeless. Do you feel that? Are you walking around like you're ok and have it all together? Are you hiding the fact that actually your heart is cold, small, and lifeless?

You're not hiding it from Jesus.

The point of Christmas is that He came to earth in order to offer you a new heart. To breathe life into you (psst... like God did to Adam and Eve in the garden when He first created people). He came to bring you quite literally back from the dead, better than any movie ending or Christmas story ever told except this one, the greatest one.

God wants to give us life. He wants to breathe His breath into us. Most importantly of all, He sent Jesus to conquer death itself so that He could give us eternal life and new hearts that will never grow cold and always have life. The next few days, we'll take a look at ways a cold heart acts and see why the only true solution is to let Jesus heal your cold heart.

Let Jesus give you His heart that was fully broken for you, so yours can be fully healed in Him.

Day 14
The Cold Heart is Bitter

Living in Boston is to live in despair due to weather for most of the year. Summer is great, but it's about two months long, if that. The rest of the year we flirt with gloomy, cold, rainy, muddy and, most of all, snowy weather. Christmas provides a brief respite where at least there are decorations and twinkle lights to mask the terrible weather.

There was one particular early spring a few years ago where it sleeted or rained for weeks on end. It got to the point that our weatherman became more of an emotional counselor than a forecaster. He said, and I quote, "This next stretch of weather is going to require psychological fortitude."

I had zero fortitude. It made me sink into despair. New England weather chews some people (me) up and spits them out covered in flash-frozen mud.

All this to say, sometimes our hearts have to endure too much. Bad things can go on for too long (things, obviously, much worse than the weather). Life circumstances, hardships, and struggles can be so trying that we no longer see any hope of change. We can grow so angry or disillusioned that it turns into bitterness, which is an emotion that burrows into our hearts. Once there, it's hard to uproot.

This happened to a woman in the Bible named Naomi. She lived during a tumultuous time in the Old Testament when no one was really in charge. There was war, famine, and violence, and in the course of all that both of her sons died before either of their wives had children.

In those times, children were your savings plan, your retirement account, your insurance. So to have none meant that Naomi was left with no real future or hope. She couldn't see a way out of her situation. She was grieving, angry, homeless and without a way to sustain herself. She even changed her name from Naomi, which means pleasant, to Mara, which means bitter.

Surely we can relate to that. There are times when it just seems too much. All of it. Too many bills, too much sickness, too much sadness, too much trauma. We lose hope. Our hearts, on our own, can't imagine a way out of the mess that life has become. Our cold hearts become bitter.

But when God is the one providing the hope, it's not dependent on our solutions or our ability to fix things. It's dependent on Him, and His hope is certain and sure.

In Naomi's case, God provided her a daughter-in-law, Ruth, who bucked all the cultural norms and, after her husband died, stayed with Naomi. Ruth should have gone back to her home country to remarry, but she didn't. When Naomi encouraged her to return to her home country, Ruth said,

> Don't urge me to leave you or to turn back from you. Where you go I will go, and where you stay I will stay. Your people will be my people

and your God my God. Where you die I will die, and there I will be buried. [Ruth 1:16-17]

She went back to Naomi's homeland (Israel) and God provided a totally unexpected and surprising new story for both of them. He gave Ruth a new husband, and they had a son. Naomi was able to live out her old age with family, care, and security. What's more, Naomi's grandson would grow up to be the great grandfather of King David, the family line from which Jesus would one day be born.

From a widow's bitter heart to the birth of Jesus – the very birth that we celebrate at Christmas. No situation is too dark or complicated or socially unacceptable that Jesus can't heal it and give you hope. The hope that Jesus gives is not a wishful feeling; it's a reality that overcomes the darkest of days because Jesus has overcome them.

Perhaps Christmas exacerbates all the things you wish were different. Perhaps you are bitter about what could have been. Perhaps you can't figure out how you could possibly experience hope. When we follow Jesus, we can be sure that His hope is real. Jesus' promises are real. Our hearts do not need to stay stuck in bitterness. Like Naomi, we can be set free from bitterness and step into a life full of true hope. Let Jesus heal your bitter heart and give you His hope.

Let Jesus give you His heart that was fully broken for you, so yours can be fully healed in Him.

Day 15
The Cold Heart is Defensive

Death, taxes and, I'll add, standardized tests. Some things are grueling yet unavoidable, and standardized tests are one of those things. We've got one daughter in college, so we've survived the SAT and ACT whirlwind once, and I have nothing good to say about the process; but, like death and taxes, my opinion will not change the reality.

When our younger daughter was in third grade, already a fluent reader plowing through chapter books a few grade levels higher, she failed a standardized test assessing, of all things, reading. The report came back indicating she had almost no reading comprehension or skills to speak of.

My husband and I were stunned. What had we missed? Where had we let her down in her education? I panicked and quickly called for a meeting with the principal. She looked over the scores, paused and said, "Give me a few minutes."

She left, while I sat in a tizzy. About ten minutes later she came back, laughing.

"You are not allowed to see the test, but I am." She gave me a knowing look.

I had no idea what the look meant, as I was not in the know.

"She missed the first line. She filled in the wrong bubble. So every answer after that was also one line off. All of her answers were the wrong bubble because of her first answer."

I let out a sigh of relief, but you can be sure I filed it away as reason #45,996 that standardized tests are ridiculous!

Our hearts are like that. Actually they are worse, yes worse than standardized tests. We get one thing wrong and then we proceed to make a small issue worse and worse until we have a full disaster on our hands.

Our daughter didn't know her bubbles were off, but we often are aware when something goes wrong and we let it slide. It's just a little thing. What's the big deal?

Because our hearts are broken, and because they are cold and lifeless, increasingly bigger and bigger mistakes come naturally to us. We see it in so many stories in the Bible, including with Israel's first king, Saul.

God commanded him to fight the Amalekites, a people group that had long been antagonizing the Israelites. He commanded Saul to attack but not to keep any plunder (just like in the story of Achan from Day 9). Saul won against the Amalekites, but he kept the plunder, including all the livestock. When the prophet Samuel asked him why he did this, instead of admitting his mistake, he dug in, making it worse.

He lied and told Samuel that he had obeyed God. But it's hard to hide the fact that you've kept entire herds of livestock, and Samuel rightfully said, "What then is this bleating of the sheep in my ear and the lowing of the oxen that I hear?" [1 Samuel 15:14]

Saul dug in again. Twice. He even blamed his own people for bringing the livestock out of the battle. Samuel finally told his king to stop making it worse. Samuel explained it was never about Saul's actions, it was about what those actions said about Saul's heart.

> Does the Lord delight in burnt offerings and sacrifices
> as much as in obeying the Lord?
> To obey is better than sacrifice,
> and to heed is better than the fat of rams.
> For rebellion is like the sin of divination,
> and arrogance like the evil of idolatry.
> Because you have rejected the word of the Lord,
> He has rejected you as king. [1 Samuel 15:22-23]

Saul couldn't stop digging in, he couldn't stop explaining away his mistakes, and he lost everything as a result.

And we will, too.

Our cold hearts will try to explain and defend and justify and lie to get out of admitting our sinful reality. We messed up. We are making it worse as we go. Our hearts can't get it right apart from Jesus giving us His heart.

When we let Jesus give us His heart, we become free. We no longer have to live in fear of being caught in a mistake, or sin. God already knows what we've done (and what we will do). When we let Jesus give us His heart, His actions are what God sees, and over time (sometimes a long, long time) those are the actions our heart increasingly wants to take.

This Christmas season we will make mistakes, we'll sin, we'll choose poorly – likely all before our first cup of coffee in the morning. It's an emotional time of year with extra complexity and many opportunities to not get it right. This Christmas instead of getting defensive when we mess up, we can relax, apologize where necessary, and move on knowing that the God of the entire universe sees the life and actions of Jesus when He sees us. No need to hide or lie. You can be at peace, real peace, if you let Jesus heal your defensive heart.

Let Jesus give you His heart that was fully broken for you, so yours can be fully healed in Him.

Day 16
The Cold Heart is Dark

Our current house (a different one from the shaving cream debacle) is a good outside party house because we have a yard, a place to play basketball, and a pool that, if properly encouraged, can heat to a fairly high temperature for those early summer nights.

We learned after the shaving cream incident though. Now when we have a larger class or school party, we often enlist a few of our friends to help chaperone, and we have large spotlights to make sure that all the kids are safely in view. Sure, we don't want them to wander off our lawn – we are surrounded on most sides by woods and swamps; but also we like to have visibility because, well, teenagers. Need I say more?

Backyard parties require light, and lots of it. At one recent party, we enlisted the help of some college guys to hold the spotlights. Having only recently been high-schoolers themselves, they reveled in finding kids on the verge of wandering off into the woods or swamp, or perhaps getting a little too close to each other in the pool. Once errant teens were spotted, they'd swing the blazing spotlight onto them to show us, and everyone in a one mile radius, what the teens were up to.

In the darkness we can't see what's real, what's happening, or what might be hiding; but the moment the light shines, everything is exposed.

That's true for our hearts as well. Our cold hearts are dark. We both can't see what is real and we also delude ourselves into thinking we are capable of hiding something we'd rather people not know about. Our cold hearts think we can manage just fine in the dark, when in fact we are likely knee deep in the swamp and headed for disaster.

This can be particularly true at Christmas when everyone is excited about the idea of festive lights and good cheer. We can play along while actually feeling the darkness of our own hearts even more. We pretend we can see what is going on, but we can't. We try to hide our sense of dread and darkness, but we know it's not sustainable. We need a spotlight, and we need it to shine directly onto our cold, dark hearts.

Jesus does that for us. The gospel of John opens by saying in verse 4 that Jesus "…is life, and that life was the light of all mankind. The light shines in the darkness, and the darkness has not overcome it." In my previous book, we took a close look at what Jesus meant when He said, "I am the light of the world. If you follow me, you won't have to walk in darkness, because you will have the light that leads to life." [John 8:12]

The bottom line is that Jesus is our light this Christmas. He shines His light on us and exposes us sneaking off into the darkness thinking no one will notice. He exposes us lost and full of dread but not wanting to admit it. He shines His light into every single crack and mess and secret thing we think we are hiding. And here is why this matters for your cold, dark heart: the darkness of this world, the darkness of our own hearts, is no match for the light of Jesus!

Once He shines His light into our hearts, we don't have to live in fear of stumbling around lost in the darkness, or of hiding our own darkness and pretending everything is okay. It's all exposed. It's all out there for Jesus to see, and He can't be overcome. Every single time, the light of Jesus wins out.

If you are feeling that the darkness is too much this Christmas, if you are lost and stuck but trying to pretend you are not, let Jesus shine His light into your heart and expose it all. Let Him give you His heart, which is the true light and leads to true life.

Let Jesus give you His heart that was fully broken for you, so yours can be fully healed in Him.

Day 17
The Cold Heart is Fearful

I have a fairly advanced fear of heights. But I'm not ready to accept it. As I type this, I can imagine many high places (the Statue of Liberty, St. Paul's Cathedral, the Grand Canyon, the Bunker Hill Monument in Boston, and multiple lighthouses of America's coast) and I feel excited. I love those places. I love to see the views from the top. I love a good climb. And I've had a totally irrational snap with reality at each of them.

When I am exposed to heights, some part of me that I don't agree with just takes over. I can't control it, and I don't even understand it as I type this in my office safely seated about three feet off the ground.

We have video of me in this state of total fear. I'm panicking and often crying. But I don't recognize the problem the moment I am back down on the ground. I often think I can try again, while my family rolls their eyes and refuses to talk about it with me.

My fear makes no sense and yet it completely takes over.

This happens to our hearts as well.

Our cold hearts allow fear to take over and grip us in a way we don't understand so that we do and say things that make no sense. Both physically, as in the case of me crab-walking along the edge of the Grand Canyon (a sight no one needs to see), but also spiritually. We let fear rule the moment. We act in ways that make no sense and are often wrong and hurtful. Perhaps even more so this time of year when tempers are short and emotions are on edge.

We can see this in the story of the disciples who had been with Jesus for some time. They'd seen Him heal people, cast out demons, interact with the Pharisees and feed a crowd of thousands with just a few loaves of bread and fish. Yet, when they found themselves on a boat with Jesus and a storm blew in, they let fear totally take them over.

> As evening came, Jesus said to His disciples, "Let's cross to the other side of the lake." So they took Jesus in the boat and started out, leaving the crowds behind (although other boats followed). But soon a fierce storm came up. High waves were breaking into the boat, and it began to fill with water. Jesus was sleeping at the back of the boat with His head on a cushion. The disciples woke Him up, shouting, "Teacher, don't you care that we're going to drown?" When Jesus woke up, He rebuked the wind and said to the waves, "Silence! Be still!" Suddenly the wind stopped, and there was a great calm. Then He asked them, "Why are you afraid? Do you still have no faith?" [Mark 4:35-40]

Jesus fell asleep and the disciples, despite everything they had seen and heard and learned, were suddenly convinced they were about to die. In other words, they freaked out. They let their fear overtake the reality that they were living with Jesus, the Messiah, God on earth in human form. They couldn't see who He really was though He was right in front of them.

They let fear rule their hearts and tell them something that wasn't true (remember the very first chapter on Day 1 – our hearts are inclined to believe the lies whispered to us).

Jesus calmed the storm with three words. Then He asked the disciples, "Why are you so afraid? Have you still no faith?" Good questions for them, and good questions for us. Like the disciples, we can know Jesus. He is real! He calls us to be His own and He knows what dangers are around us, what chaos looms like a storm on the sea. He alone can command our fears to be silent.

The reality is, this Christmas Jesus is bigger than our fears. He offers us His heart that has already seen and experienced the very worst things: our sin and the punishment of death. He experienced it and He overcame death itself. It is with that power that He can give us a heart that does not need to fear.

We don't need to lash out or freak out from fear. We simply need to know that Jesus silences the storms, calms the waves, and, if we follow Him, our hearts are safe in His keeping. Let Jesus calm the fears of your heart.

Let Jesus give you His heart that was fully broken for you, so yours can be fully healed in Him.

Day 18
The Cold Heart Denies Truth

Okay, so it's December 18 if you are reading this in chronological order, which means you may or may not have your Christmas shopping done. If you have a tween or teen girl, they may have asked for jeans. Here's what you need to know: the phase of the super high-waisted jeans, the mom jeans, cannot last much longer. I've been writing about this small bit of fashion horror for a few years now, reminding people that in the early 90s we fought, and won, to get jeans that did not make us feel like we were wearing a corset. We fought for mid-rise jeans that allowed us to, say, eat a large meal, perhaps with dessert, and still be able to breathe.

It's so clear that high-rise jeans are ugly and uncomfortable, and yet the hipsters, the trendsetters, the teenagers insist these cages of denim are in fact worth wearing. The truth is obvious and yet they deny it. (It is my Christmas wish that by the time this book is published this fashion wrong will be righted.)

Of course we do the same thing, and we do it with much

more at stake. When our hearts are cold and dark, it's easy to just make up our own idea about what is true and deny the very obvious reality. Things that are bad for us, we call good. Things that we say we won't participate in, we find reasons to be part of. Promises we make, we decide to break.

Truth becomes relative in service of our cold hearts, and it's an awful way to live.

Just look at the story of Peter, one of Jesus' main disciples. He was given to putting his foot in his mouth, and was slightly impulsive, but he was a devoted follower who left his life as a fisherman to pursue the teachings and life that Jesus offered.

Yet he denied Jesus. Jesus even warned him this would happen, saying, "Peter, let me tell you something. Before the rooster crows tomorrow morning, you will deny three times that you even know me." [Luke 22:34]

Peter couldn't fathom doing such a thing, but in the end, when Jesus was arrested and taken away to be crucified, Peter knew the truth about who Jesus was and yet totally and completely denied it.

> So they arrested [Jesus] and led Him to the high priest's home. And Peter followed at a distance. The guards lit a fire in the middle of the courtyard and sat around it, and Peter joined them there. A servant girl noticed him in the firelight and began staring at him. Finally she said, "This man was one of Jesus' followers!" But Peter denied it. "Woman," he said, "I don't even know him!" After a while someone else looked at him and said, "You must be one of them!" "No, man, I'm not!" Peter retorted. About an hour later someone else insisted, "This must be one of them, because he is a Galilean,

too." But Peter said, "Man, I don't know what you are talking about." And immediately, while he was still speaking, the rooster crowed. [Luke 22:54-60]

The story is recorded in all four gospels. It's a powerful reminder that we can't heal our own truth-denying hearts. Three times people asked Peter if he was an associate of Jesus, a disciple, a follower. The answer should have been yes, yes, and yes. But each time, though Peter knew the truth, he flat out denied it: no, No, NO!

That may be how you feel now. You want to believe what Jesus says, after all it's Christmas and you'd like it to be about something real, true, and good; but following Jesus comes with a cost. People will notice and ask you, "Aren't you with that man?" It's so easy to let our cold hearts whisper there may be another way to answer, a more culturally acceptable way, an easier, less demanding, or less scary way.

Our hearts apart from Jesus simply don't know what to do with the truth. We need Jesus to take our hearts and give us His. Give us His heart that found Peter after the resurrection and restored him to a life of great faith and service as one of the foundational leaders of the church. We need Jesus to give us a heart that is full of boldness and joy – that won't worry about what the culture says their version of truth is.

Denying the truth of who Jesus is will only make us fall further into a life we don't actually want. This Christmas, let Jesus give your heart the truth. It's Him. He is the Truth.

Let Jesus give you His heart that was fully broken for you, so yours can be fully healed in Him.

Day 19
The Longing Heart

I'm annoying to be with while watching Jeopardy. I get that from both my dad and my husband. We all have weird, obscure knowledge filed away that makes us experts – if only to ourselves. Dad is good at old movies, history and hard sciences. My husband can rule sports, math and economics. I'm best at religion, fiction and popular culture.

Jeopardy is thirty minutes where, if the categories swing your way, you're brilliant, well-rounded, and frankly you can't imagine why everyone isn't impressed. Unless it's a category you don't know. Like old movies, for me. Or ornithology of eastern Iceland. Then you feel dumb and worthless. The existential highs and lows of game show trivia – so many emotions are wrapped up in knowing the answer (or the question, as the case may be).

While Jeopardy thankfully turns off at 7:30 p.m., the questions about life are often only beginning to swirl around in our brains as each day ends. They are the questions about purpose, safety, love, and family that keep us up at night.

Wondering. Questioning.

Habakkuk was a prophet in the Old Testament who had a lot of questions. He saw how his people were behaving. They were following idols, not God. Why were his people falling into idolatry (again)? Why did they choose the wrong path (again)? He knew that if they continued, God would allow the people to be captured and taken into exile. How would that help anything? He had deep questions about the very existence and identity of his country.

So he took his complaints to God. In fact, the book of Habakkuk is a series of his questions and God's answers. One part that is sometimes overlooked is what Habakkuk did after he asked his questions to God. He said,

> I will climb up to my watchtower
> and stand at my guard post.
> There I will wait to see what the Lord says
> and how he will answer my complaint. [Habakkuk 2:1]

This image Habakkuk describes is that of a watchman climbing up his tower to look into the distance for the first sign of a messenger coming (call it ancient near-eastern email). The image is one of waiting. Our culture has taught us to believe that everything can be done quickly, but the truth is often we have questions and the answers are not immediately apparent. Sometimes we just have to... wait.

When God did answer him, it likely wasn't the answer Habakkuk expected.

God detailed the coming invasion and explained how it would point to the ultimate restoration of the Jewish people. Then God said,

> Write my answer plainly on tablets, so that a runner
> can carry the correct message to others. This vision
> is for a future time. It describes the end, and it will

> be fulfilled. If it seems slow in coming, wait
> patiently, for it will surely take place. It will not be
> delayed. Look at the proud! They trust in
> themselves, and their lives are crooked. But the
> righteous will live by their faithfulness to God
> [Habakkuk 2:3-4]

An answer like that can be hard for us. God's timing is not our timing. Maybe His answers seem slow to us as we wait. Habakkuk would see his country invaded, his people taken into exile, and they wouldn't return for close to 100 years.

But living by faith means our hearts can trust God's timing.

Perhaps this Christmas you have some unanswered questions. Your heart may be longing for an answer that is not clear to you. It may be a practical question about a job, school, or house, or it might be a spiritual or emotional question like "how did this happen" or "what is next in my life?" You can bring all your questions to God and He will answer; but you may have to wait.

There is one answer you will never need to wait for. At the deepest level, our questions are answered in the person of Jesus. Following Jesus may not cause a sign to pop up on your computer that says which job to take, but trusting Him with your heart will allow you to live faithfully until that answer, and all answers, are clear. You may wait on your watchtower for hours, days, years or perhaps a lifetime. But you will not wait alone, and you can have certainty that the answer "will surely take place."

The next few days, we'll look at how a heart that is longing can attempt to fulfill those longings in wrong ways. But we'll see that the only true solution, if you are worried and consumed by unanswered questions, is to let Jesus be your answer.

Let Jesus give you His heart that was fully broken for you, so yours can be fully healed in Him.

Day 20
The Heart is Longing to be Whole

I'm not sure if this generation really loves the *Indiana Jones* movies the way my generation did. I know they released a new installment in the series this past summer that didn't live up to the hype, but back in the day everyone knew the lines, everyone got the jokes, and many of us wanted to be Indiana Jones (whatever that looked like for a teenage girl in the 80s). Who among my generation was not terrorized by the Nazi's face being melted off? Or who didn't wish they could snap a whip around while fending off shooting arrows, rolling boulders and strategically placed skeletons that shot out from walls?

One of the many lines that has stuck with me was when the side-kick kid, Short Round, asked Indy what the Sankara stones were. Indiana, summing up the pursuit of treasure hunters, evil empires, and corrupted archeologists seeking power and immortality, answered, "Fortune and glory kid, fortune and glory."

Of course in the movie Indy found the remaining stone and, after all sorts of plot twists, returned it to its people so the stone could rest where it belonged, where it was designed to exist, no longer plaguing the world with some unknown catastrophic power.

This familiar plot has played out in movies and books across the years. Some powerful object, or critical piece of knowledge, or special person, is taken out of the place it, or they, belong by the bad guys. They take it for the fortune and glory they believe they'll receive from possessing it, but in doing so they unleash unintended, and often world-ending, consequences. The peace and order of the world can only be restored when the object, knowledge, or person is returned to their proper place – reunited, and made whole.

It's a story that is played out over and over because it's the condition of our hearts, and it's the story woven throughout the entire Bible. From the very beginning when Adam and Eve were sent away from the garden, our hearts have longed to be healed and returned to that place where they were whole. We see that in the history of the Israelites throughout all of the Old Testament. First they were slaves in Egypt longing to leave and go to the promised land, and later they were sent into exile in Babylon because of their continued idolatry. Once there, they longed to return to Israel. Psalm 137 details this longing.

> Beside the rivers of Babylon, we sat and wept
> as we thought of Jerusalem.
> We put away our harps,
> hanging them on the branches of poplar trees.
> For our captors demanded a song from us.
> Our tormentors insisted on a joyful hymn:
> "Sing us one of those songs of Jerusalem!"
> But how can we sing the songs of the Lord
> while in a pagan land? [Psalm 137:1-4]

They were longing to return to the land God had given

them, and yet their own sin had forced them out. They were unable to feel whole, at home, or at peace, because they weren't where they belonged.

Eventually, Israel did return to Jerusalem. There was a partial healing of their broken hearts, but it wasn't full, because they, like us, had hearts designed for a garden, a city, a land that we do not yet live in. We long to return to what God began in the Garden of Eden.

We are out of place, we are not where we belong; and if we let our broken hearts rule us, we will pursue our own fortune and glory to the detriment of ourselves and those around us. We long for a wholeness that we cannot achieve. But Jesus can. He can give us His heart and He can complete and fulfill that longing because a relationship with Him is what we ultimately need to be whole.

During this time of year it's easy to go after the wrong things, trying to satisfy the longings of our hearts with all the festive trappings of the season, or perhaps with an extra level of business and distraction – our own pursuit of fortune and glory.

But a misplaced longing to be whole will lead to emptiness and frustration. Only by following Jesus can our hearts truly be whole and at rest in this world, even as we know that our own promised land is being prepared. Let Jesus give you His heart that makes you whole because He is wholly true.

Let Jesus give you His heart that was fully broken for you, so yours can be fully healed in Him.

Day 21
The Heart Longs for Restoration

In 8th grade we let our older daughter get a few blonde highlights in her otherwise honey brown hair. It was a mere strand or two, nothing major. My girlfriend, who is our hairdresser, promised it would be subtle. And it was. They were beautiful highlights just around her face. (Parental warning: a few subtle highlights leads to a head of platinum blonde hair in about two years).

At the same time, we'd just purchased a new "fast curler" for the girls of the family. It was a strange looking device with a chamber that opened, sucked in the piece of hair to be curled, did something magical, and then spit the hair back out curled and lovely. We'd had a few solid practice rounds that had met with success.

Naturally, our daughter decided to try it with her newly blonde strands.

But, in this case, it sucked in the blonde strand and promptly jammed. Instead of hair coming out magical and curled, smoke began to wisp into the air and the smell of something burning filled the room. I yanked the plug out of the wall but there was no yanking of the hair. It was firmly in the chamber, curled up, smoking and attached about two centimeters from our daughter's face.

I'm not sure there are words in the English language to describe the feelings that were felt at that moment. The only thing our daughter wanted was her hair restored and back to normal, but it seemed that all paths led to some scenario where her hair melted into the curler or would have to be cut.

She longed for restoration, and yet only difficulty and damage seemed to be in her future.

In the Old Testament we see the same sort of deep longing (albeit a few thousand years before electric hair curlers would hit the scene) in Nehemiah, an Old Testament book about a Jewish man who had risen to a place of prominence during the exile of the people into Babylon and even worked directly for King Artaxerxes as his cupbearer. As mentioned in the last chapter, this was during the time when the Israelites longed to go back to Jerusalem. The book opens when Nehemiah was given a report about Jerusalem, learning some bad news.

> "Those who survived the exile and are back in the province are in great trouble and disgrace. The wall of Jerusalem is broken down, and its gates have been burned with fire." When I heard these things, I sat down and wept. [Nehemiah 1:2-4]

Nehemiah's heart longed to see the city rebuilt and restored. The walls of the city were a physical symbol for the people of Israel. Without walls, there was no city; and without the city, their identity was still a people in exile. Nehemiah's heart wouldn't be satisfied until the walls were restored.

He was given permission to return, but when he got there, restoring the walls was a complicated and hard process, both physically and spiritually. There were people who opposed his work and undermined the restoration efforts, who cared about their own identities more than their exiled people.

What Nehemiah longed for, and what we all long for, is to have a restored heart and a restored relationship with God. But like our daughter's hair in the curler, there is no actual way we can achieve that on our own; we cannot restore our own hearts.

Often at Christmas we try to fix what is broken with slick wrapping paper and expensive gifts, laughing a little louder at the office party or donating more shoeboxes to the church fundraiser. We try to restore what we know is broken in our hearts by doing, acting, pushing and scrambling.

But our actions are not enough.

After about 10 miniature screwdrivers, a mallet (truly), and YouTube tutorials, my husband was able to free some of our daughter's hair, but some melted and had to be cut. Nehemiah managed, after about 13 years, to make the city safe and fortified, but the people still wandered off to idols and pagan practices. Stone walls can't actually restore people's hearts.

We long to be restored and yet nothing we do can accomplish that. Only Jesus can. He offers us His heart that is restored not because He waved a magic wand or had the best Christmas card photo, but because He took the brokenness and the damage and the mess we made, the broken walls of our hearts, and paid for it to all be restored with His life.

By offering us His heart, the very thing we long for can now be part of our identity: a truly restored heart.

Let Jesus give you His heart that was fully broken for

you, so yours can be fully healed in Him.

Day 22
The Heart Longs for Fulfillment

I've lived in the woods, or wooded areas, most of my life with only a few years of city living. In all those years, nearly 50 of them at the time of this writing, I'd never seen an owl. I'd heard them. I could identify them easily, Barred, Great Horned, Screech, etc.; but I'd never seen one. And I so badly wanted to see one. My friends see owls like some people see crows. I only see, well, crows.

Then one day, while taking the trash down our driveway, there was a rustle in the bushes to my left. A blur of motion shot in front of me, and then more rustling occurred in the trees to my right.

It all happened so fast, but when my brain caught up to my eyes I yelled (to no one at all), "It's an owl!!" I was able to see it perched in the tree. I even took a picture.

Then, since of course I posted my blurry, early morning picture of the owl online, my neighbor wrote to me and said, "Oh yeah, that's a Barred Owl. She lives in our yard and has a nest with three babies! Come by and I'll show you!"

Suddenly I went from zero owls to regularly watching a nest of owlets grow up. I was awash in owls. I had a parliament (I looked it up) of owls within regular and easy viewing. My longing to see an owl had been fulfilled and then some.

We read about another longing that was fulfilled in the story of Zechariah and Elizabeth in the gospel of Luke. They were older and had been unable to have children. One day, when Zechariah, a priest, was working in the temple, an angel appeared to him and announced that he and Elizabeth would have a son, and they were to name him John.

Zechariah was unsure that he could believe this incredible news. The thing they had longed for all these years was happening? It seemed impossible.

Zechariah asked the angel, "How can I be sure of this? I am an old man and my wife is well along in years." [Luke 1:18]

Because he doubted the power of God, the angel made him unable to speak until John was born; but Elizabeth was overjoyed. "How kind the Lord is!" she exclaimed. "He has taken away my disgrace of having no children." [Luke 1:25]

In the next chapter of Luke, Mary learned that she was pregnant and carrying Jesus – the Messiah who everyone had been waiting for! She went to visit Elizabeth, and the two of them were full of joy and wonder at this amazing turn of events in both of their lives.

But here's the interesting thing. Yes, Zechariah and Elizabeth's greatest desire was fulfilled. Yes, their son, John the Baptist, would know Jesus in person and prepare His early ministry years for Him. But John would grow up to be beheaded by King Herod, and Jesus would grow up to be crucified.

Sometimes the things we long for most – the things that we think will fulfill our hearts – are also things that will bring hardship and pain in this life. Jesus died so that that sort of hardship and pain will ultimately be gone forever. He conquered death itself in the resurrection, but note: He didn't bring John the Baptist back in this life. He didn't spare His own mother, family and followers from seeing Him suffer horribly during His final days before dying. Nor did He prevent the suffering that would come to those who followed Him over the years.

Jesus doesn't promise that if we give our hearts to Him that He will make our lives instantly easy and better. If our dreams of fulfillment include perfect health or great jobs or fabulous families at all times, we will not find fulfillment. At the core of our broken hearts, our deepest longing can only be truly fulfilled in Jesus.

Christmas has become all about fulfilling wishes and dreams. Sometimes, like my owls, your dreams can be fulfilled; but nothing can truly fulfill the wishes and dreams of our hearts that long to be healed from broken lives and a broken world, except Jesus. Let Jesus fulfill your heart's deepest longing, and, even when the hard things of life come, you will be fulfilled in Him.

Let Jesus give you His heart that was fully broken for you, so yours can be fully healed in Him.

Day 23
The Heart Longs to Act

Some people are talented at drawing or computer science or quilting or cooking or animal training or singing or playing any instrument they touch. They have talents that are obvious and remarkable, and we all marvel at them. But some of us have more obscure talents.

Mine is my ability to hold my breath and dive deep under the water. You can see how this has almost no practical value as I plan my family dinner each day or make sure my child's poster board for science class is the snazziest. Underwater skills also are not useful in carpooling, dog walking or anything that has to do with being a sports mom.

Yet, I'm not only good at it, I love it. I am instantly happy and at ease if I am a good 15-20 feet underwater, and preferably with a task to complete. This has come in handy at our family camp on Lake George in the Adirondacks where I've become our mooring setter over the years. Give me a set of pliers and some chain or shackle pins, and I can set a mooring for boats, jet skis, rafts, and floats.

Or throw some golf balls into deep water and I'll happily spend the morning retrieving them like a well-trained golden retriever; and, obviously, anytime I can snorkel in more tropical waters I am like, well, a fish in water! Sure the snails and small lake bass of Lake George are interesting, but parrot fish and sea turtles are utterly amazing.

I love it and I'm good at it. I've gone pretty far down both in the lake and the ocean, and the deeper I go the calmer I feel.

Except, I've gone too deep.

I've done what I know I'm capable of and I've messed it up. I've blown vessels in my eyes, I've triggered terrible migraines at the base of my skull, and I've gotten "mask squeeze" bruising around my eyes. (I'm super fun to take on vacation!!)

I long to use what I know my talent is, but in this lifetime I can't fully do that without danger or harm.

Our hearts are like that. We long to live the way we know we were designed to live way back in the garden. Our hearts long to live unbroken lives. Our hearts long to act the way they were designed to act.

The Apostle Paul writes about it in his letter to the Romans. In chapter 7, he has a long (I'm just going to say it, Paul can be wordy) section on knowing what he is meant to do: wanting to act on the things God calls him to and yet facing limitations because he is still a broken person who sins.

> I have discovered this principle of life – that when I want to do what is right, I inevitably do what is wrong. I love God's law with all my heart. But there is another power within me that is at war with my mind. This power makes me a slave to the sin that is still within me. Oh, what a miserable person I am! Who will free me from

> this life that is dominated by sin and death? Thank God! The answer is in Jesus Christ our Lord. [Romans 7:21-25]

Our hearts, no matter how much they long to act in the right way, are broken. On our own, apart from following Jesus, we cannot will ourselves to be better. I am 100% sure I can dive deeper, but my body will not allow me to do that without breaking. Not in this lifetime.

Our broken hearts betray what those same hearts long for. That tension is where we live. That tension is what makes us anxious, angry, sad, and miserable – perhaps especially at Christmas when we long to make it all perfect and good and whole. But as Paul concluded, "Thank God! The answer is in Jesus Christ our Lord."

When we let Him give us His heart, we can act with goodness. We can act with joy and peace. We can act with real cheer and real generosity because we are acting under the power of Jesus' heart. It's the only way we can truly be free from the longings of our hearts, which fall so far short of their goal. It's the only way we can truly act in love, and this Christmas, it's the only way our hearts' longings can be satisfied.

Let Jesus give you His heart that was fully broken for you, so yours can be fully healed in Him.

Day 24
The Heart Longs for Life

One of the great skills that comes with being a mom is the ability to stalk my children. This became apparent when they first started going to overnight camp and I realized there was a webcam looking out over the swim area. I would watch the camera online and zoom in. *Was that my daughter? Did she have a pink bathing suit? No, that was last year, this year it was purple and white. Wait, was that her?* When I'd finally spot her, I'd screenshot her image and announce, "I have proof of life!"

One year I learned she was taking a scuba diving class from the webcam. Her letter came a week later announcing, "I'm signing up for scuba diving. I think you'll be excited about that!" I was excited, in fact I'd been watching her walk out of the lake, tank and tubes attached, around 11 a.m. for the past five days.

More recently, our older daughter spent half her summer studying in the Middle East, and each morning I'd check the "find my phone" app when I'd wake up in Boston. Was her phone at least where it was supposed to be? The app couldn't tell me if she'd fallen down an ancient well or become lost in a cave system, but it could tell me that, all things equal, she was still there. Still alive.

Granted, technology makes it easier (crazier?) these days, but the general need to check on people, to know they are ok (or aren't) is built into our very hearts. We long for life because we are designed for life. When that longing for life is not met, it is the deepest way our hearts can be broken.

Remember, when Adam and Eve were sent out from the garden, they were sent out from a world that had not experienced death. Death became part of what it meant to be human at that time, but it was never natural. It was never in the original design, and we feel that every day.

Mary Magdalene felt that after Jesus died on the cross. She felt the wrongness of what had happened, the wrongness of Jesus dying. She went to the garden where He was buried because it's all she knew to do. Her only option was to grieve the wrongness of death itself.

But when she got there, instead of finding the body she found an empty tomb, and instead of finding a dead person, she found proof of life.

> Mary was standing outside the tomb crying, and as she wept, she stooped and looked in. She saw two white-robed angels, one sitting at the head and the other at the foot of the place where the body of Jesus had been lying. "Dear woman, why are you crying?" the angels asked her. "Because they have taken away my Lord," she replied, "and I don't know where they have put Him." [John 20:11-13]

When she turned around, Jesus was standing there. She saw Him! And talked to Him! And the life she had longed for, both for Him but also for herself, was fulfilled right there in front of her. She ran back to tell the disciples that she had seen Him, that He was alive. That death, which had been part of the very fabric of the human experience, had met the beginning of its end in the person of Jesus.

If nothing else is true at Christmas, I know this: our hearts long for life.

Sometimes we use the holidays as a way to hide the dark truth that we can feel death. We feel it in our bodies as they age, in our families as they fracture, and in our minds as we try to reason with this grim reality. We try to cover it up this time of year with more of everything, yet we find that death is still there.

But so is the Author and Perfecter of Life. Standing there before us, like He was with Mary at the empty tomb. Not pretending death isn't real, but defeating it. That's right, Jesus overcame death itself and lives eternally right now. Right as you are reading this. And He offers that same death-conquering-never-dying-again-life to us. He offers us His heart that has done the work on our behalf. Yes, we'll die in this life, but never, ever again.

If you're honest, that is what your heart longs for. We long for life because it is how God made us to be. Jesus stands in front of us and offers it to us. He offers us His heart which is life eternal. He offers us proof of a life that will never end, never die, and never be broken again.

Let Jesus give you His heart that was fully broken for you, so yours can be fully healed in Him.

Day 25
The Healed Heart

Well here it is! It's Christmas and we've solved all the problems of the heart, and now your life will be perfect!!

Ok, or not.

Probably someone is already stuck in traffic, or has to return a gift, or can't make it to your dinner, or, even worse, they CAN make it to your dinner. Maybe it's pouring rain and the kids are restless or the dog threw up, or perhaps you're totally alone wondering if anyone will call you (or maybe you are thrilled to be finally alone!). There is a distinct chance that at least one of you is reading this locked in your bathroom because it's the only peaceful place in the house and you are re-thinking all the chocolate you put in the kids' stockings. Even though it's Christmas Day, and even though we've spent 25 days talking about how Jesus heals our hearts… we aren't there yet.

Jesus doesn't expect us to be. In fact, He knew how all this would go, and He said, "I have told you these things, so that in me you may have peace. In this world you will have trouble. But take heart! I have overcome the world." [John 16:33]

Troubles? Yes. Even on Christmas!? Yep.

But Jesus says to take heart – not because of anything we can do, accomplish, or even contribute to. We take heart because He has overcome the world. We may not feel it in full right now, but that doesn't make it any less true. When we let Jesus give us His heart, we join Him in what He has already overcome – all the things we've looked at these past four weeks: the brokenness, the misguided ways we go, the cold and dark actions we take, and the longings we so desperately want fulfilled.

Jesus takes those hearts, our hearts that believed the lie, and He heals them. Like all healing, it can take some time. We're in this world and there is still trouble (we still cause trouble), but the heart Jesus offers us is healed, it is whole, it is His.

You do not need to live with a broken heart. Not one more day. You do not need to believe the lie whispered in the garden any longer. You can live in the hope of the gospel, which is a story about God (not you), but a story that He invites you to be part of, right now, on this Christmas day.

Let Jesus save you by admitting your heart is broken. When you let Him give you His heart, you will be healed. You will begin to experience life the way God designed it to be from the very beginning.

That is the hope and the reality of the story of the Bible, and it is the real reason you can truly celebrate Christmas today.

Let Jesus give you His heart that was fully broken for you, so yours can be fully healed in Him.

THE HEALED HEART OF CHRISTMAS

Acknowledgements

Is a third book like a third child? I don't know, I only have two daughters, but I do feel like this book got dragged to a lot more meetings, road trips, and games. It got pulled out and scribbled on here and there and then stuffed back into the folder.

There's been a lot of change since my last book, including jobs, churches, dogs, life stages and oh yes, a pandemic. Sometimes I thought I'd just quit. All of those things were so important and required my attention. But I always felt like God was saying, "Nope! Keep going." So I did, it just took a little longer.

This book is what we in church-land call a topical book. My first two were more exegetical books, which is a fancy way of saying they followed in the order that the Bible verses unfold, verse by verse, with a linear progression.

Topical is not my natural habitat. I am a happier Esther when teaching and writing exegetically. So I struggled, until I wrote my friend and mentor, Pastor Ray, and asked him how he did it.   (He's been preaching and teaching for decades, and his 30 plus books are a balance of both styles). He wrote back, and I have to quote him to do his advice justice. He said:

> As for the exegetical part, just remember. No. One. Cares. I'm smiling as I write this because I know you care, and I get it. But there's nothing wrong – and much to commend – to start not with the text per se, but with the sorrow of our unhappy world, and then to bring the hope of Christ's coming to it.
> -Pastor Ray

And that's what I tried to do. I tried to start with my own heart when I am unhappy, and with what I believe to be true in those cases – Jesus *did* come and He *has* healed my heart! I'm not perfect, and I'll probably be writing "Stressed at Christmas" devotionals forever, but I know Jesus is real and true. Pastor Ray was right, sometimes you just need to hear about the hope of Jesus.

Thank you to my Dad, George Lawrence, for being my Editor of Theological Correctness and Tone, and to Bryn Limmer for being my long-suffering Editor of Details, Punctuation and Hipness. And I'd be remiss if I didn't thank my Voice of Reason, Emily Roth, for making magic happen in formatting (page numbers don't just add themselves!) and generally laughing through life with me.

Of course thank you to my girls, Abby and Riley, for allowing me to put our lives on display. Lastly, and always, thank you to my husband, Les, who always encourages me and has been a great example of what a healed heart looks like during an especially tricky past few years. (Also he's generally much nicer than I am at Christmas. It's fine, snarky people write more books).

This is a crazy world, and it's been a wild few years, but our hearts were broken long before Covid hit the scene, or people became so polarized, or you voted for this person and I voted for that person. This Christmas it is my prayer that you will let your heart truly rest in Jesus because He is the only way your heart can ever survive all this. Not just survive, but be healed.

Esther Baird, September 25, 2023
www.estherbaird.com

Made in the USA
Middletown, DE
27 October 2023